Clothes for every season

Susan Thomas

Oxford University Press

We wear different clothes for
different seasons.
This book will tell you about them.

Contents

The four seasons

winter

spring

Winter is the coldest season.

Winter clothes keep you warm.

The weather gets warmer in spring.

In summer it can be very hot.
You need clothes that keep you cool.
In autumn it gets colder.

Clothes for winter

Winter is the coldest time of year.

You need to wear a warm coat.

Gloves can keep your hands warm.

It can be cold inside, too. You can wear slippers to keep your feet warm.

Clothes for spring

It starts to get warmer in spring.
But the weather can change quickly.

Sometimes it rains in spring.
You need a waterproof coat.
Wellington boots keep your feet dry.

Clothes for summer

In summer the weather can be hot.
Cotton clothes keep you cool.
Cotton is a thin material.

The sun can be very hot.
You can wear a sunhat to protect your head from the sun.

Clothes for autumn

Autumn can be cold and windy.
Jumpers keep you warm.
You might need a coat.

These children are out at night. They wear scarves and coats to keep the wind out.

The weather changes

Sometimes the weather can change suddenly.
This man is dressed for a cold day.

When the sun comes out he
takes his warm coat off.
What will he do if it rains?

Index

Oxford University Press,
Great Clarendon Street,
Oxford OX2 6DP

First published by Oxford University Press 1997
ISBN 0 19 916929 2

Available in packs
Clothes Pack (one of each title)
ISBN 0 19 916934 9
Clothes Class Pack (six of each title)
ISBN 0 19 916935 7

Acknowledgements

Illustrated by: Alex Brychta (p2), Claire Pound and Terry Burton(pp14-15).

The Publisher would like to thank the following for permission to reproduce photographs: John Birdsall (p9); Magnum/Harry Gruyaert (p13); The Telegraph Colour Library/Sarah Hutchings (p11).

Cover illustration: Terry Burton.

Cover photo: John Birdsall.

Printed and bound in Hong Kong